Overtime

BOOKS BY JOSEPH MILLAR

Overtime
Fortune
Blue Rust

Overtime

Poems by
JOSEPH MILLAR

Carnegie Mellon University Press
Pittsburgh 2013

Library of Congress Control Number 2013937142
ISBN 978-0-88748-586-2
Copyright © 2001 by Joseph Millar
Printed and bound in the United States of America

10 9 8 7 6 5 4 3 2

Overtime was first published by Eastern Washington University
Press in 2001.

First Carnegie Mellon University Press Classic Contemporaries
Edition, June 2013.

Cover design: Eden Weingart
Original cover design by Scott Poole
Original cover photograph courtesey of Miriam and Ira D.
Wallach Division of Art, Prints, and Photographs. The New York
Public Library, Astor, Lenox, and Tilden Foundations:

Hine, Lewis. "Two Workers Repairing Machinery," Empire State
Building Photographs

for my father

CONTENTS

ONE

TWENTIETH-CENTURY LANDSCAPES:1
TELEPHONE REPAIRMAN:3
ED'S AUTO REPAIR:4
YOUNG MOTHER:6
OAKS CARD CLUB:7
FIBER OPTICS:9
TAX MAN:11
SPANISH BLUES:12
SELLING OUT AT THE TOP OF THE WORLD:14

TWO

SITTING BULL IN CANADA:18
THE WAYWARD CARPENTER'S APPRENTICE:20
AUTUMN RAINFALL:21
STRIDER:22
AFTER LISTENING TO A LECTURE ON FORM:23
NAMES I'D FORGOTTEN:24
LIGHTNIN' HOPKINS RETURNS HOME:25
OUTSIDE MONTEREY:26
DECK BOSS:27
HEART ATTACK:29
KEATS' SHADOW:31

THREE

NEAR THE CONTINENTAL DIVIDE:34

KUNG FU:36

FILIAL PIETY:37

MIDLIFE:39

MY FATHER AND THOMAS WYATT IN HEFKA'S BAR:41

HANSEL AND GRETEL'S FATHER:43

SOLE CUSTODY:44

FAMILY THERAPY:45

FOUR

POEM FOR A NEW GIRLFRIEND:48

LOVE PIRATES:49

FAT CITY:50

SECOND-HAND CLOTHES:51

WORK SONG:53

AT BAY MEADOWS WITH ROBERT HERRICK:54

SUNDAY NIGHT:56

LISTENER:57

DARK HARVEST:58

WAKING UP AFTER READING PROUST:60

"Time to ask pardon of everyone."

—*Villon*

ONE

TWENTIETH-CENTURY LANDSCAPES

We are down on our knees in the cement vault below Harrison Street
listening to the big cable slither toward us through the pipes.
All day the long trucks have unloaded their pallets of steel
onto the cracked asphalt above, while rain soaks the walls
of the Granny Goose potato chip plant
and the line crew tabulates the minutes of overtime,
collecting the pull-ropes and fish-tapes
and coiling them into the truck bed.

Most of us are thankful.
Soon this cable will be in and we can travel,
speechless and half awake, back through West Oakland,
past the stained doors of the transmission shop on Cypress
and the blotched facade of St Vincent de Paul, the ripped tarp
flapping from its porch like a trapped angel, the cracked tiles
of the Chinese movies shining in the rain.

In our homes we will eat cheeseburgers and sweet corn
while the news channel flickers, the sound turned low,
over tableaus of athletes bathed in million-dollar sweat,
and the wrecked landscapes of Bosnia freezing in the dark.
We watch the hollow-eyed women, speaking
in fractured bursts, their hands fanned open in mute appeal.

It's a hard war to figure out.
Fascism's humped shadow presses down,
smashing Arabic fountains and mosques, passing over
steep valleys bristling with land mines,
cleansed human cinders darkening the snow.
Why doesn't someone do something, we wonder.
The cameras slide back over bodies of new Cadillacs
and something pushes us further toward sleep.

Certainly it's daylight in Bosnia by now.
Unshaven men, shifting in the cold, turn away
from the C-Span floodlights. The corporation our president
works for stays awake always, watching the Dow Jones
dance with the bond market, and tomorrow we'll be back
under the street, easing our way toward an early lunch,
dreaming of overtime, talking baseball.

TELEPHONE REPAIRMAN

All morning in the February light
he has been mending cable,
splicing the pairs of wires together
according to their colors,
white-blue to white-blue
violet-slate to violet-slate,
in the warehouse attic by the river.

When he is finished
the messages will flow along the line:
thank you for the gift,
please come to the baptism,
the bill is now past due:
voices that flicker and gleam back and forth
across the tracer-colored wires.

We live so much of our lives
without telling anyone,
going out before dawn,
working all day by ourselves,
shaking our heads in silence
at the news on the radio.
He thinks of the many signals
flying in the air around him,
the syllables fluttering,
saying *please love me,*
from continent to continent
over the curve of the earth.

ED'S AUTO REPAIR

When I bring the car in for brakes
everybody's out front eating donuts,
one of the children jumping
from the stack of tires by the door,
wearing a hat that says Fast Orange.

Edward's out back in the shop
welding the exhaust on a blue Chevelle
and mumbling to himself. I thread my way
past a Pontiac engine block balanced
on the black tines of a forklift,
a gold Cutlass with the driveshaft
hanging down in front,
to watch his torch flame splash
its lizard shapes onto the dark steel.

I'm not often permitted entry to this dim cool mine
smelling of gas and iron
where the air hoses hiss in the corners,
sparks spray onto the floor,
and everything seems combustible
as though the fire in the Cadillac manifold
leaning against the wall
still glowed under the rust.

Edward's smooth Hawaiian face, greasemarked
under one eye when he peels off the goggles,
wears a half-smile, his hair matted down
with ashes and dirt,
the big vein on his right hand
shining with sweat. What's up,
he says, turning toward me,

while Vulcan, his grandfather,
misshapen god of the forge,
slides through the shadows under the muffler,
the new metal ticking
as he breathes on the weld.

YOUNG MOTHER

Someone should take her picture
right there under the Bud sign,
uneasily eyeing the slight wrists of the waitress
bringing grilled cheese and soup.
She's trying to have a quiet lunch,
hair pinned evenly back from her face,
nails painted red and flat shoes crossed at the ankles.

There are jagged gaps of hunger constantly opening
in the skin of the world. Imagine the great breasts,
veins branched under the flame-shaped stretch marks,
nipples chapped and starting to leak when the black
newborn two booths away starts to wail.
Three years out of high school, her milk lets down
toward the wispy voice, while she looks on,
embarrassed, easing her body forward
over the pastel formica. Whose mother is she?

The lips of the homeless man by the bridge
unfasten from the jar, now drained of its wine,
as he waits for the rivers of sleep to carry him down.
And the hitch hiker standing alone west of town
watches the tall wheat bend on the wind,
remembering the blanket covered with stars
she wrapped him in at bedtime.

She's everything we need in her loose skirt from Penney's,
the sun spreading out on the table top and her water glass
casting its blossom of light sideways over the floor.
She leans forward, eyes narrow, watchful and tense,
tears into the sandwich like a dog. The new milk clotting her blouse

OAKS CARD CLUB

They bring their hunches and combinations
to these trancelike rooms with no windows,
where they'll be called guests
and summoned by name
to the sessions of Hold 'em and Five-dollar Pan.

It's five A.M. and the Gold Room's buzzing.
You're forty feet above the blackjack table
changing out the paging speaker,
hoping you don't drop your wirecutters
on the aging blonde in a cowboy hat
slouched behind four stacks of chips.

This is the only time they'll permit you to work here,
and you must move in silence on your perch
but you can see the highball straw
the woman's chewing and the hairless
smallboned hands of the dealer.

Later you eat pancakes in the lounge
surrounded by eight TV's replaying
highlights and scores from last night.
You're trying to decide if you feel lucky.
Smoke hangs like a beckoning ghost
over the studious Asian, caged at his window,
counting out new hundreds
to a winner wearing Ray-Bans and a Phillies jacket.

When you step outside, you're surprised by the sun,
half dazed on the crowded sidewalk, the eyes
of the mailman on San Pablo Avenue

distantly fixed in the morning haze
like the face cards you might someday hold in your hand
or the lights on the lift truck at quitting time.

FIBER OPTICS

On Labor Day the last barbecue smoke
        had drifted into the branches,
and Public TV showed the legendary strike
                  at J&L Steel in Aliquippa,
the cops opening fire
        on the worker's picnic, the men in shirtsleeves running,
the women, some carrying children, falling in the Pennsylvania dirt.

I'm thinking about this,
        driving my new truck down Highway 280,
getting twelve miles to the gallon on the company credit card
                with a storm coming in from the west.

We're working nights and week-ends pulling wire
        into the ceilings of Silicon Valley,
moving our ladders just ahead of the drywall crews
        with their knives of adhesive,
                their radios blasting Metallica,
the carpet gang in the finished wing
                spreading beige-colored glue on the floor,
nobody talking, hurrying along in the midnight glare of the heat lamps.

Impossible anyone here would strike,
        though we're comrades of sorts,
                and hungry for something,
listening to rain pound the glass doors
        of this palace paid for
by venture capitalists, whose appetite nobody questions.
        Inside it's a hardware bonanza: boxes
of galvanized fasteners overflow onto the Visqueen tarp
                that covers the stairs like a membrane.
Somebody squats by the telephone switch,

wiring teflon patch bays into brilliant steel racks,
  and testing each pathway
    the delicate voltages follow.

Everybody wants to work, the more hours the better,
especially the young ones, snowy with gypsum dust, wolfing their lunc
  on a stack of new two-by-fours
while the overtime keeps piling up
    like valet parking behind the first tee
where the owners and union reps, weekday afternoons
    gather to discuss trade.

Outside the trenches and conduits slowly fill with water
and two of us crouch in a low cement box,
    adjusting the filament cable,
the fiberglass link that feeds the big hubs.
And nobody's wondering about Karl Marx or the poems of Cesare Pav

We're trying to stay down out of the wind
and close up the resin-filled splice case
  so the ghostlight signal can travel across,
sending its neuron-flickering code
    as fast as a man can think.

TAX MAN

Thunder Bob used to drive for Consolidated Freight
before the small bones began to press
against the nerves in his lower back
and his right foot went numb.
Now he slouches in blue suspenders,
forearms propped on a steel desk, doing my taxes.

In the den his wife watches the Simpson trial
and he wants to get me done, squinting down
at last year's forms, muttering, a Chesterfield
burning away between his fingers. You need
more write-offs, he says, peering sideways
through the smoke. Since you can't afford a house,
why not have another kid, eh?
Rain blowing in off the bay rattles the windows
and the branches of the pin oaks moan. He knows
my wife moved out last year. The kids I've got
are waiting, eating cold Chinese by the TV.

You watch, he tells me. Soon they'll start messing
with Social Security. I can hear the lawyers' voices
carping down the airwaves and I think sometimes
the rain will never end, a bleak mudcaked creature
prowling the landscape, entering our homes
while we sleep, its ragged breath like quicklime
misting our faces.

Driving home through the storm I think of him
leaning against his porch, telling me
to be careful. Try to kick down more cash
into Retirement, he'd said, bracing himself
on his good foot. Nobody knows for sure
what the hell's going to happen.

SPANISH BLUES

"I want to weep because I feel like it,
pronouncing my 'name, Federico Garcia Lorca,
on the shore of this lake ..."
                    Double Poem of Lake Eden

Late afternoon in the Hayward marsh
I had no desire to speak my name
as I sat in my patched raingear
reading about the life of Lorca.
Not to the gravel thrown up on the banks
or the egret feathers and guano
and not to the fox who came out of the reeds,
red fur streaked with tidewater,
who glanced at me sideways and vanished
in the rough grass of the estuary.

Watching its small tracks fill in the failing light
I felt my body settle deeper,
remembering things I'd stolen—
money, flowers, the red tool box—
and never told anyone;
kindnesses and love betrayed,
nights of false promise whispered
into the ears of believing women,
their children eyeing the door while I packed.

There was no gypsy music like his
rising from the hills of my childhood—
no tree of song branching up from the earth
with guitars that hovered like birds of prey.

And I was no solitary horseman
with olives in my saddlebags
kicking up dust on the narrow road.

But as I squatted in the salt marsh,
the lights of a tanker winking on near the bridge,
I felt this desire to sing about death
and to praise the deep pools and shoreline
of the fallen landscape that held me.
Three days past the end of my fiftieth year
the tide lay slack on the Hayward flats,
its husks of dead starfish trapped in the mud
and the sky turning dark as the sea.

SELLING OUT AT THE
TOP OF THE WORLD

For John C.

Nobody spoke in the Arctic cold those mornings we rode
over wrecked lunar fields following tracks to the dynamite shed.
                    Not the drillers from Oklahoma in ski masks
and insulated coveralls, not the Eskimos from Barrow,
some wearing only down vests and flannel; not even us,
                    the survey helpers, tears and snot
                            from the freezing wind lacing our faces in ice

We'd screw the cans of explosive together, load the steel chain
and transit and start driving north to the line,
                    where leads of dark seawater
flexed through the ice like a wound that refused to heal.
Scrabbling across sloped pressure ridges and planting
                    wire flags in the crust,
we knew our charts would someday be sold to Nixon's cohorts,
Exxon and Richfield, that the Revolution had come north
                    to freeze under the waters of Prudhoe Bay.

                    Scattered across the north slope
of the Brooks range, countless gypsy seismograph crews
                    scratched and gouged in twilit shadows,
prospecting the ocean floor. The ice where we lived grew
six feet thick over the Beaufort Sea, and we clustered like flies
                    at the top of the world, watching the sun
creep like a slow fuse partway around the horizon, soft light shining
back from the surface, hanging the air with ghosts:
                    mountains upside down
at our feet, white buildings hovering half out of the sea,
and the moon on its back, refusing to set
                    over the ragged plains.

If our hearts had been pure we'd have grieved
            for ourselves or found other wages farther south.
Instead we surrendered to spasms of laughter in the anaesthetic cold,
            making up names for the Texas bosses:
Black Jack, Sidewinder, Big Tomato; planning the movie
we'd someday write, a noir-Western starring Richard Widmark's
            pale narrow eyes and rictus grin.

Wyatt Earp and Jim Bowie had nothing down on our Okie drillers,
who'd flown here from the Middle East with stories
            we listened to evenings of jewelled
            Arabian sunsets or the withering
sandstorms of Egypt, where Moslem laborers
            were called back to work from their prayers
                        by numbers they wore on their backs.

Here we only stopped work to wolf candy bars
            or piss in the frozen tracks of the boom truck.
Nobody wanted to say much about home, though one spoke
of the Sacramento delta where he'd worked as a brakeman
            for Southern Pacific, gone to high school
with the Mitchell brothers before they became pornography kings.
Some were here to escape other lives, ex-wives and children,
            jail time down south,
many just back from Vietnam. Who knew if they'd watched the live
demonstrations where people like us dodged tear gas, the walls
            of our communal houses on fire
with Che Guevara's austere face or the thunderbird of Cesar Chavez?
            Here the Indians never gazed straight
at anyone white and the stiff wings of winter closed
down on us all, as though we'd been born without histories
            to this godless landscape of ice and bent light.

When we got loose in town we paid whores from LA a hundred extra

to dine with us in the Gold Rush Room of the Anchorage Westin Ho
I fell quickly in love with mine, her black nails sparkling
                    like onyx rain
as she turned her wrist to look at her watch.
They harvested our amnesiac wages the way pipeliners
                    empty an oil field.
No one could wait to sell out for a fortune, be rid of the Sixties'
experiments—ecology, brotherhood, socialism—except maybe
                    the cook from Baton Rouge,
who'd lost fifteen grand playing dice at the Embers
and wanted us to help get it back.

                    Not much would ever be given back
to the wilderness beginning to crack and thaw over the bright seams
of moonlight near the drilling rigs on the sea. Not the underground
                    swamp gas rising through cleavages
forced apart by the drills, not the patches of tundra scarred
by surveyors trying to leave tracks in the storm,
                    not even the ridges of this winter's ice,
                              glowing like quartz in the tractor lamp

When we returned camp was moving again, exhaust fumes
hanging the air like a shroud, two D-8 Cats towing trailers on sleds
                    over ashen terrain toward Canada.
We watched from above in the company chopper, hovering over
the dim caravan, eating chocolate and taking quick swigs of scotch,
                    the smell of death frozen into the night,
fuel oil, diesel smoke, leaf-mold pre-dating
the kingdom of Solomon, the collapsed insides of the dinosaur,
                    the decomposed skull of the mastodon
turning the cold steel rotors of time
                              under the blind April stars.

TWO

SITTING BULL IN CANADA

It's three years since Little Bighorn,
        the Month of Blackening Cherries;
Crazy Horse has been murdered
and civilization keeps rinsing its glittering face in the dawn,
        perfecting the treaties and blueprints,
while the railroad pushes its stained fangs
                west through the rivers of grass.

By now, from under the whispering skirts
        of the pale women who bore them,
Hawthorne and Poe have come forth, haunted.
Whitman leans over a Long Island bridge
        trying to keep his shadow from frightening the fish,
and across the Atlantic,
Swinburne is paying London whores to dress up like police
                and whip his bare flanks with a strap.

Sitting Bull listens to the ravens
        folding their wings in the pines,
his village of women and old people turning over in its sleep.
There's no place left, he thinks,
        watching the charred thorns of autumn fly upward,
a thick-bodied man leaning back in his lodge,
                its skin walls sighing in the wind.
There's no word for "art" in his language,
        though he'll pose on the stages of Cody's Wild West show,
the bonnet of carnival feathers flowing back
                in the copper daguerreotypes.

Maybe he wonders if anything around him
        means what he thought:
                evening, his horses, the buffalo;

and prays for a great storm to tear it all down.
Maybe the blind flowers of Sade and Baudelaire
        open their rank petals over him as he dozes,
too tired to look out at the stars,
            lying on his left side,

                            facing away from the fire.

THE WAYWARD CARPENTER'S APPRENTICE

The apprentice has trouble sleeping nights
when the westbound freights come rocking past,
his body anchored to the black tools padlocked
into the bed of the new truck in the driveway:
the chisels and carbide sawblades lying side by side
under the chalkline's aluminum cone, and the windings
of the drill motor wrapped in their tight still coil
waiting for morning.

The high whistle cuts through the fog,
startling the gypsy moths chattering at the porch light,
and embeds itself in the thighs of the Levi's
hanging on his door. Things will never be the same.
The bottoms of his workshoes want to wander off
by themselves, and the sweatstains growing cold
under the arms of the orange T-shirt
begin to dream they can fly.

He has bills to pay and turns fitfully, trying to swim
deeper down the underwater canyons of sleep.
But the baseball hat, dusty with sheetrock,
is remembering stories about seaman's papers,
the starlit archipelagoes of the restless Pacific.
And down in the truck, the leather gloves
lie stiff on the dash, one tar-splashed hand
pressed against the windshield,
waving goodbye.

AUTUMN RAINFALL

She makes her supper late, moving slowly
in the bare kitchen, between the entertainment channel
and the glass tray of leftovers bubbling in the oven.
The wind pushes on the outside walls
and the floor joists creak as she wanders
aimless, unsure of her hunger.
She sags onto the stool near the heat vent
resting her face on her palm.

To be brave is to be tired much of the time,
half stunned by the continuing dusk.
She sets out the plate and the single glass
because it's time for the next thing—
the day-old casserole, its pinched edges
starting to burn.
She feels her lower abdomen cramp
in the stillness under her housecoat;
and for the moment it takes her to rise,
she thinks of nothing.
The dark photographs of childhood
bear down from the walls
and the veils of the rain
tear open over the trees.

STRIDER

For James J.

Early each morning Jimmy ran
through the East Cleveland projects
over broken glass
past the wrecked stores and buildings
where the welfare families lay, folding their bodies
deep into the gases and haze
rising like sleep from the city.

He came charging up Euclid Avenue
on fifty-year-old legs,
Afro streaked with gray,
past the Opera, past 150th Street
breathing after fourteen miles in steady bursts.

No voices urged him on and no one waited at the finish,
except for the gashed Chevrolet by the curb
spewing upholstery ticking
or the Arab at the Convenient Market
who never gave credit to anybody.
He couldn't see the smoke stack
far below by the black river
that burned like a torch through the dawn.

AFTER LISTENING TO A LECTURE ON FORM

I'm afraid of the mountains
in this thin glacial air,
of going to sleep in their shadow,
that the granite inside them
and the threads of bright metal
may not hold once the night comes.

I'm afraid of so many people talking,
the cat smile of the poetry scholar,
his ridged skull.
When he spoke of measure
I could feel my wristwatch tighten,
remembered the payments coming due
on my daughter's tuition.

I went down by the horses.
Birds were walking in the hay
beside the feet of the Appaloosa.
He looked at me sideways
in the swaying dusk.
The wheels of his jawbones,
the great vein in his face.

Sometimes I can hardly breathe.

NAMES I'D FORGOTTEN

I used to get drunk in the morning, starting awake
in the sinister warmth of the couch, tangled up
in my raincoat and pants like a trapped animal.
I'd follow the rusted-out tracks to the store,
ignoring the alien mothers with laundry, the crows
on the trash bin, the cryptic remarks of the grocer
looking out at the rain, asking when it would stop,
smiling as he slid the fifth into its narrow bag
like a man loading artillery. The day would flare briefly
and disappear, its singed dust prickling my scalp.
I'd listen to gravel trucks snarl in the alley, the crows
with their bandaged voices, my oldest child
calling my name from the shadows 3000 miles away.
And study the streetlight's fractured reflections
like stars whose names I'd forgotten.

LIGHTNIN' HOPKINS RETURNS HOME

Maybe it's the rough voices we admire most
wearing their bondage lightly
and chanting their raw spells into the air
under a gray trance of sky.

The country lay below him like a woman
when he looked from the railroad trestle
carrying the worn suitcase
and watching out for snakes.
He listened to the whistle die away
beyond the fields, stepped across the fencewire
through the canebrake east of town
as though entering a church.

He sat down gazing at the feed store's porch,
the hound asleep in the Texas dust,
and the sad mule standing by itself—
gathered them into the shadows
behind his dark glasses, 'til the blues
began to pace forth
like mourners at a funeral:
Money Taker, Mr Charlie,
Bald Headed Woman, Shine On Moon,
bowing slowly to each other
over the bridge of the old guitar.

OUTSIDE MONTEREY

Outside Monterey the highway
runs by the sea and the torch singer
on the radio has a voice like twilight:
"I couldn't love you more, child,
if time was running out..."

My ten-year-old shaved his head when his mother left,
looked oddly more adult last night,
coloring the Stay Out sign for his bedroom door.
Earlier I stopped to buy goldfish, dinner
for the snake he keeps trapped with its hunger
in a glass box.

Night drifts into the artichoke fields
and the swallows veer off toward the hills,
bent wings scissoring the dusk.
I park under a tree, lean back
with the lights off and the engine running.

I want to travel all night like this,
the ocean whispering beside me in the darkness,
passing no one on the road.

DECK BOSS

For Mike N.

There was a big run that year, salmon the color
of silver and diamonds tumbling in over the transom,
their bodies nudging your thighs and waist
where you stacked corkline in the fog
with the seabirds crying overhead.

You could imagine the down payment
on a house in the woods, the groceries piled on the table,
and the eyes of your first child waiting to emerge
from the hips of the woman you loved,
her full skirts opening over waves of grass
following the inland breeze.
On slow days between openings
you sat alone by the reel, sewing new panels
into the net or taping splices
in the tie-up lines, studying the water.

There wasn't much time for thinking,
the afternoon the wrench kept dropping in the bilge,
the replacement transmission balanced
over the driveshaft on two ropes, the boat drifting down
on a sandbar, the skipper yelling to hurry it up.
And maybe you forgot for a moment
about becoming a father
the night we made three sets in the surf
and the wave broke through the windows
knocking out the electronics and the stove.

We put in two hundred thousand pounds by mid July,
eating Dennison's chili and oatmeal for breakfast

and suggesting names you might consider.
Mostly our own, but others as well:
Algernon, Guinevere, Rufus,
watching the net on its way to the surface
under the daylight moon,
like a body struggling to be born.

HEART ATTACK

You've always suspected the voice of defiance
would carry you only so far, wondering
when your life might end
even as you lounged on the high school steps
smoking a Lucky Strike.
In those days you considered it honorable
to make yourself drunk with fear,
climbing the abandoned cement plant's silos
or driving flat out with no headlights over the river road,
while Buddy Holly's "That'll Be the Day When I Die"
spilled all summer from dashboard speakers
in the slow fat days before Vietnam.

And you never outgrew the thrill of resistance,
the reckless desire to be stricken with dread.
In the Halloween parade years later,
wired on amphetamines and port wine,
you became afraid to look off to your left—
while the scarlet candles and black paper skulls
fluttered and spun through the wind—
at the spot where Castaneda says
the angel of death walks beside you,
trailing one wing like a bandage into the autumn smoke.

Now you're listening to a ragged cough
on the far side of the curtain, your neighbor
cursing in tremulous Spanish, his moan
like the dirge of some Catholic ghost.
You're trying to make a deal with God,
whispering an embarrassed farewell
to red meat and cigarettes,
to your insolence and pitiable hauteur.

You're wired to a twelve-volt electrical harness
under a stiffening veil of dried sweat, your chest
a patchwork of shaved gray stubble,
ribcage plastered with ultrasound gel.
You're not seeing much in the way of a vision
unless it's the fractured sand-colored light
stuttering from your hospital TV

where a lone outlaw rides for the Texas border.
The posse's closed off the canyon behind him
and the sunlight's falling in clots through the trees.
He's splashing his horse downriver,
trying to cover his trail.

KEATS' SHADOW

I could be in Hampstead, I'm thinking,
instead of this Oregon hayfield,
with my collar turned up in the front seat, the river
passing almost in secret, behind dim veils of spring rain.
The life of Keats I've been too overcome
to continue lies open on the dash.
Its fourteen-year-old grieving his mother's death
has crept behind the teacher's desk to hide
and I can see a blue heron standing, hunched
and solitary near the blackberry canes, keeping watch.

Keats doesn't have much time. In four years
he'll be a grown man, a poet without prospects
in the savage world, except for the bright flame
of his fellowship, an apothecary's license, and his pen.
He can write at the foot of a staircase,
at a side table in someone's parlor, or in the garden
of a strange hotel, reading Shakespeare and Milton,
the ocean wild, tearing away at the land.
Oddly-lit stars pulse through his nights like fireflies
on the brim of an old hat
while he reinvents the sonnet and the ode

and the jackals of poverty and death fold their paws
and settle down to wait. He learned to live gracefully
under their gaze *without reaching irritably after fact*
while Wordsworth pretended to ignore him
and his brother wasted slowly away. Keats knew
the blossoms that come riding out
once the sap starts to rise in the tree.
He knew how the tall grass darkens and bends,
how the heron croaks through the April rain
and nobody tells what things mean.

THREE

NEAR THE CONTINENTAL DIVIDE

I said goodbye to my father in a black Oldsmobile,
unwilling to park and linger, waiting for the flight
to Pittsburgh. It was August, almost time
for his classes, and the mountain sky was clear
over Denver as I herded the big car down
through the switchbacks, leaving the airport behind.
That night I camped by a stream in the foothills
named for a saint I'd never heard of.

I don't think he'd planned on dying any time soon,
stumping through the terminal doors in moccasins
and shorts, the end of a dead cigarette in his teeth.
He'd insulted my poems as usual,
eaten his pork chops and eggs, leering
at the waitress when she brought the Bloody Marys.
Before he got out of the car he'd stuffed two fifties
into the ashtray and told me to keep firing.

When I was twelve I didn't want to be President
or King of England. I didn't want to be in movies
like my children do, lying dazed in the TV's astral glow
listening to the guitars. I wanted hair on my arms
and big shoulders. I wanted to be a man like him,
draped in mystery. A cigar and a hat flecked with rain
singing "If I Loved You" on the way to work, or leaning
against the Turf Club bar, relaxed and elegant,
the Racing Form in one hand and a whiskey in the other,
gazing down at the horses and sighing, "Christ, Mac,
would you look at the wanton splendor of it all."

That night in the Rockies, jumpy from five days
of drinking, I couldn't sleep, listening to the darkness.
I'd wanted to tell him about the wild mustangs
at Pyramid Lake, the Northern Lights crackling across
the Yukon, ask if he thought they might be angels,
ask if it hurt him that I never came home.

My father was six miles above the earth,
Melville's *Typee* in his lap, wedged into an aisle seat
and calling for another gin, the lights winking on
across the wing: red, right, returning,
and his hat pulled low
over the yoked forebones in his skull.
The next day I would drive west through deep canyons
into the splintered light of Utah,
electric dust rising from cracked blue hills
where nobody knew my name.
Whatever it was he gave me, in the early years
after my mother died,
that fierce kindness I'd required
to believe in the world's sudden reckonings,
was mine now. In a few months
he'd be gone.
Reagan would be President
and I'd be struggling, bankrupt, divorced.

But that night the stars came down close to the road
like the eyes of the coyote
as I cut across Nevada,
remembering how we collapsed in the snow
when the Steelers lost the title,
and laughing to myself through the darkness
all the way back to the coast.

KUNG FU

The children sit quietly on the grass,
having untied the bell from the cat's collar
so he can stalk the night moth
jagging past us in the dark,
and I'm trying not to think
about the blue walls at the Detox Center
where I left their mother this morning,
shivering and clutching
the bestseller about vampires,
a broken suitcase at her feet.

I'm sitting in the doorway
watching the night drift into the yard,
the low voice of the news channel
running like water behind me.
Overhead the pine cones have cracked
partly open and the hooked branches
rake the late breeze like a claw.

The youngest kneels on his skateboard,
looks up at me and says
he wants to learn Kung Fu
before school starts next month,
to wear black and carry
its invisible weapons in secret,
moving softly through the fifth grade
like a spy.

FILIAL PIETY

For Andrew and Chuck

I never wanted to know what was under the bed
in that room by the stairs on Walnut Street. The rain
spattering the windows and the black shutter knocking
in the wind. Fossilized licorice and a Three Musketeers
turning slowly into chalk, two pages from the comics
of *Johnnie Mac Brown* or *Lash Larue,* and the unnameable
dust blossoms gathering and growing like the tumors
in my mother's breasts. These had taken her
six months before and left us alone with him.

He drank whiskey all through that summer,
volumes of Donne and Herbert stacked on the rug,
as he sat in his bathrobe on the spavined couch
or prowled unsteadily through the upstairs rooms,
breathing scotch vapors into the darkness
like a ruined furnace.

We'd turn our faces to the wall, feigning sleep,
refusing to look at that ravenous grief. Instead
we stoked the childhood fires that still glowed
through this exhausted theatre.
Come morning we'd ride bikes to the cove,
clothesline lariats coiled at our waists
and break Coke bottles against the pier.
We stole apples and gum from the corner store,
hid out striking matches under the bridge
or climbed up the barnacled rocks by the harbor,
skinning our ankles and tearing our jeans.
We fled through the days without looking back
until twilight darkened the neighbors' back yards
and we'd creep through the gate, past

the soft wisteria draped on its trellis,
the garbage can half-filled with rain.

We'd spy on him then as he sat in the lamplight,
his book lying upside down in his lap, resting
his face on the same flat palm that had slapped us
that morning or else stroked our hair. He'd be
listening to his crackly Sibelius records, weary,
drunk, complex and unshaven, and willing
to forgive any trespass to avoid being left alone.

MIDLIFE

She's slim and seems distracted, the social worker
who visits my apartment, who wants to know
why my ten-year-old was alone New Year's Eve
when the cops came through the door.

His mother was drunk, I say, and I was up north
with my girlfriend who doesn't want any more kids.
Would she like a cup of tea?
We do have some problems here, I know —
as I forcefeed old newspapers into the trash —
but hopefully nothing too unseemly,
no disarray that can't be explained.

I want to say I've tried
to find another way to live,
away from the electric metal wires
that whisper to me in the afternoons,
the snake dreams that follow after,
uncoiling slowly in my sleep
and the supermarkets where I go unconscious,
humming to myself and staring, minutes at a time,
at the olives and loaves of bread.

There's not much to show for all this:
four rooms, a dented Olds, tattered pictures
of Che Guevara and Muhammed Ali,
the Sixties with their fire and music
scattered like highway cinders. Does the State
offer therapy for aging single fathers?
Is it all right to smoke?
Would she like to step into the back where it's dark

and fuck, standing up amid the laundry?
She smiles vaguely, hands me her card,
says she won't need to return.

Later I think this must be what it is
to get older. My knee hurts getting up
from the couch. Can't work like I used to,
and my chest hairs are turning gray.
I'm angry with my son, now quietly asleep,
for needing help with everything: homework,
breakfast, rinsing the shampoo from his hair;
and sad, as I gather his small raincoat,
the baseball hat saying Surf's Up,
hang them over a chair, and start washing the pot
of day-old spaghetti we ate for dinner.

I listen to Miles with the lights off,
knowing the phone won't ring any more
and too tired to shower. I listen to my breath
leave and return, rain falling
into the cold trackless night,
and the wind in the trees outside
like someone passing.

MY FATHER AND THOMAS WYATT IN HEFKA'S BAR

He was awful to service people when he was drinking,
this renegade literary child of the rich,
his family inheritance long since spent,
announcing his exile from the common man
in a strange quaint language, silvered with alcohol,
calling the waitress "Charming lass"
like some toss-pot Elizabethan roué.
I'd be too ashamed to look at the woman,
silently wishing I'd never come home,
that I'd stayed where I was, milking the overtime
painting houses or shoveling fish.
Sometimes it was dangerous, like the night
he was waving a tennis racket by the jukebox
in O'Brian's Roadhouse. They were ready to kill him
in his seersucker jacket, his knit tie askew at his chin.
I still don't know how we made it to the car.

One Christmas I found him pounding the bar at Hefka's
with three unemployed miners muttering ominously
in the bruised light by the shuffleboard game.
The frayed elk was glaring down through the smoke,
nostrils flared in warning, antlers glazed
with nicotine and shellac. I perched beside him
on a torn red stool by the jars of hardboiled eggs,
the slow fan prickling my scalp.

But that night was different. The talk
at the bar flowed on as before
and the shuffleboard players turned away
as the tables began to come alive with the dayshift
from Bethlehem Steel. By midnight Johnny Cash

was rumbling sorrowfully into the haze,
I'd won three beers playing darts, and my father
was quoting Wyatt, his voice drifting easily
over the iambs and into the chapped face
of a teamster from Elder's Ridge.

Maybe they let it pass that time
because they could tell we were father and son
and the backlit Santa by the phone booth
smoking a fake Dutch Masters cheroot
protected us as we stumbled with our six-packs
over the frozen mud to his car.
It had started to snow and my father was singing
"Heart of my Hearts" in the front seat,
jubilant and half-redeemed by this company
of working men, by the free one
the Polish bartender slid toward us just before closing.

HANSEL AND GRETEL'S FATHER

On days when the small boy now asleep
asks me for money and movie tickets
I can't see any escape. I want to banish
playgrounds, the circus, and all bright colors
and I don't want to hear anyone laugh.
If I don't get this electric bill paid
something bad will happen.

Bottlecaps, water guns and X-Men cards
are scattered all over the homemade fort
in the garage. A Fred Flintstone mask
hangs from my truck antenna
and it's almost time for me to go to work.
I'm yelling at him
in front of his wide-eyed friends
and he sobs, sitting on his bicycle
with his hat on backwards.

He may never understand this fierce satisfaction,
watching him eat vegetables at supper,
as though the green stalk fibers and the juice
were entering my own body.
Have some more, I mutter,
the shadow behind me pressing me down
into my own dark footprints.

I don't think the woodcutter wanted gold
or even the manic afternoon sex
his witch of a wife might have promised
if he would only get rid of the kids. Probably
he just wanted to make enough
to feed everybody.

SOLE CUSTODY

Today he'll ride his bike to Safeway
in his death's head earring and mismatched socks,
where the checkers all know his name. He'll buy
Cheeto's and Kool Aid before coming home to bathe
in the rusty light from the TV, until I get off work
and collapse on the fake velvet sofa, a double order
of fast food bleeding grease through a bag in my fist.
He hasn't eaten anything green in a week
and I see the dirt under his fingernail when he points
to the surfboard he drew on his sneaker.

What would we do if I got fired, I wonder,
listening to the wind outside and the evening's lead story
announcing more layoffs in the South Bay. There's enough
in the bank for his school clothes, and the rent's
almost paid again. I should be happier.
He's been watching the talk shows. Have
you ever done it with someone you didn't love,
he asks, his old guitar resting against the wall
like an abandoned girlfriend, and the pleats
of the hound's-tooth fleamarket slacks
gathered around his small waist
like the leaves of a sunflower calyx.
Eat slowly, I say, as he smiles at me
around a mouthful of fries, points the clicker
at my chest and says I'm getting fat.

We're bound together like sailors, swaying across
a dark ocean, resigned to each other's odd humors
and unable to see the stars overhead,
as we stagger around in the engine room
of a ship with a foreign name.

FAMILY THERAPY

My brother's brown eyes narrow
when I tell him about the money
I stole to pay Christmas bills,
the lies I told the IRS and the bursts
of cruelty to my son,
how close I came last week
to picking up a drink.

He slides the five-eighths boxwrench from its case
and leans under the hood,
tells me to pry up against the alternator.
This belt's too loose, he says.

An evening breeze rustles down the pavement
as my niece comes out of the house,
long hair draped beside her face,
and leans against the fender.
Go back inside, he tells her.
Bring us a Coke. Then he turns
on me. Fuck
the government, he says.
Do you want to starve? He swipes
at the grease on his forehead
and the big knuckle on his right hand
bleeds down onto the wheel well.
Back off some on that pry bar
or we'll break this goddamn thing.

The pale fists of the hydrangea bump
against the fence and a light

comes on in the kitchen, its glow
sifting onto the driveway
as his wife opens the screen.
Everybody yells at their kids,
he says quietly,
tightening the bottom bolt.
Get in and start it up.
We need to go for a ride.

FOUR

POEM FOR A NEW GIRLFRIEND

I'm driving down the highway in the dark
on my way to pick you up,
with the ocean on one side
and raindrops spattering the windshield,
balancing a Coke between my legs.
If a baby were asleep in the front seat,
nothing would wake it,
not the hiss of the long grass
waving by the sea wall,
not the cypress branches groaning in the wind
or the dim necklaces of surf
tumbling onto the sand.

I'm afraid to do anything sudden
on this wet pavement,
afraid to change direction or speed up,
to give you the small bracelet
I bought today in the Castro
or to say anything about the future,
as though the car might slide sideways
or the doors fly open.
So the baby would go on sleeping,
a pale shadow beside me,
stirring slightly perhaps, its hands
like stars in the glow from the dash.

Impossible to tell
what snowlit oceans
might be swaying under its eyelids,
with no cars on the road
and the lights out front
all turning green in the rain.

LOVE PIRATES

I follow with my mouth the small wing of muscle
under your shoulder, lean over your back, breathing
into your hair and thinking of nothing. I want
to lie down with you under the sails of a wooden sloop
and drift away from all of it, our two cars rusting
in the parking lot, our families whining like tame geese
at feeding time, and all the bosses of the earth
cursing the traffic in the morning haze.

They will telephone each other from their sofas
and glass desks, with no idea where we could be,
unable to picture the dark throat
of the saxophone playing upriver, or the fire
we gather between us on this fantail of dusty light,
having stolen a truckload of roses
and thrown them into the sea.

FAT CITY

For San Francisco

Outside the manhole near China Basin
after pulling cable all afternoon,
unwinding the black-jacket copper
one foot at a time
                from the city's dark ovaries,
and watching the office girls hurry past,
glancing sideways at their profiles in the plate glass,
I don't want to be anywhere but here, on the sidewalk,
smelling french bread
              while the sun goes down.

Behind me, the blue stairs of a church,
a peroxide hooker waving to someone
              climbing onto the streetcar.
All the women I have wanted since I came to work today
will soon be combing their long hair down
into the night unpinning its skirts
              over their hallways and doors.

The fat pigeons hustle for popcorn
under the benches of South Park
and even the homeless man by the bridge,
hunched over the cage of his shopping cart,
has a fifth of tokay
              ablaze in his fist like a star.

SECOND-HAND CLOTHES

We've walked here from our small hotel by the park
having flown into town from two different cities.
We've washed the love-brine from each other's eyelids,
the electric airport dust from our hair, and the fluids
caked like memory from our bodies' archways,
leaving us bleached and faded, transparent
on the dazzling sidewalk, peeled eucalyptus bark
fallen everywhere in the southwest desert light.

You pick through the rack of five-dollar dresses,
a rose-printed gown held up to your waist,
half turned from the mirror as though
in a trance and I start to disappear into the morning
cast loose like some wayward ghost.
I try on a cowboy hat, pull it down low,
hook my thumbs in my belt like Jesse James,
aware of the slender manager, his cat's eye ring
on the glass display. I try on
a vest with embroidered lapels,
the black beret with a sequin in front.
I look like a Thirties Parisian jazz drummer,
a sideman for Sidney Bechet.
I'm Gerard de Nerval in a velvet bow tie,
I'm Django Reinhardt or Arthur Rimbaud
slouched in my insolent shirtsleeves.

I'm coming apart in the dust-riddled glow,
the lion-tamer's lamé boots on my feet,
a plum-colored wig falling over my shoulders,

the chorus girl's feathers caressing my neck.
I'm trying on earrings and purple eye liner,
the long satin gloves wrap me close in their arms,
with your dusky voice whispering,

It's all right, from inside the jeweled box of veils.

WORK SONG

Love picks its way through the gravel ruts
leading into the job site, past the truck tires
exploded nearby, the crows' rusted voices, black
wings and feet, cottonwoods risen in ghostly
fields and the levee's blond lip folded over
the water. It seeks itself in random orders:
pale mist settling on marsh grass, freezing

the tattered glittering webs, ragged forsythia
strewn down the fence, raindrops fallen like worlds
without end into the distant river. The job
runs smoothly, ahead of schedule, feeder frames
built in the ceilings, underground cable
punched down and tagged. See the tiered
ladders set in place, wire spools threaded

side by side onto a length of steel pipe. See
the apprentice in line at the roach coach waiting
for everyone's coffee. You know somewhere nearby
chaotic traffic fractures the April dawn. That the
Dow Jones ratings your paycheck depends on
cluster like blind spores swarming their prey.
That the homeless have wandered the hacked edge

of nightfall scavenging Pepsi cans. But here pairs
of carpenters level the windows and new tilework
arches its reverend glaze over the fireproof doors.
A fine rain glows in the threshold where your crew
hunches over the floorplan: four Benedictines
in speckled light, cowled in frayed sweatshirts,
Carhart jeans, copying out last night's changes.

AT BAY MEADOWS WITH ROBERT HERRICK

Me and Herrick are down at the end
of the Turf Club Bar drinking gin and limes,
just before the start of the final race, a two-bit claimer
for fairgrounds crows who haven't won since last fall,
when the brunette vamp three stools away
finally turns and asks for a light.

Herrick can't take his eyes from the lace
frothing at the throat of her blouse, the soft pleats
of velvet thundering away from under the sheen
of her cinched purple belt. The hand extending
the BIC lighter's flame trembles in the smoky air,
and I'm thinking he'll have to be somehow distracted
before he ends up like last night, on his knees
in the ladies' coatroom, smelling the dappled cashmere
and stroking the dun-colored gabardine.

The truth is I'm tired of watching out for his ass,
listening to stories of milkmaids and elves in the Devonshire
countryside outside his church. I haven't had a winner all day,
playing combinations of speed-ratings and chalk,
while Herrick can't miss,
betting fillies whose names end in *a*.

By now the flag is up and they're off,
Herrick's Julia, the two-horse with Russell Baze up,
going straight to the lead in a cloud of dust
and smoking the rest of the field, wire to wire,
including the favorite I'd bet with both hands,
trying to get back to even.

I can see him now,
at the cashier's window, brunette on one arm
and his hat cocked back in a kind of sloe-eyed amazement,
as though trying to remember the glittering morning,
his brunch of mimosas and scrambled eggs,
and the twilit roses of late afternoon
falling like losing tickets
in this ruinous prime of our lives.

SUNDAY NIGHT

This is my first time trying to make beef stew
and I remember the Indian stories
about thinking kind thoughts while cooking,
staying close to the land where you live,
how to lie down in its hills and pay attention.

If I don't save out the vegetables, they'll turn to mush.
The smell drifts into the ragged yard,
lifting the small hairs on the marigolds,
and the sky starts to darken.
A cricket sings by the porch. The voices
of Navajo women in the kitchens of New Mexico
float off toward the canyon. Come morning
they'll be dusting corn pollen
onto their children's tongues
so they'll listen quietly in school.

I dump in the onions, carrots and potatoes
and stand in the door with the lights off
like a man in a cave.
A snail's track glitters on the sidewalk,
dew seeping under the grassblades.
The thin bones of the gartersnake
carry me down.

LISTENER

The woman with her face pressed against my chest
and both legs locked around my knee, breathing deeply,
has floated into some quiet stream, swaying past
its wooded banks without me.

Somehow I've told her everything, whispered it
through my cracked voice into the stillness around her
as we sat in the gloom waiting for the movies to begin,
and later by the bridge, watching dim surf ignite offshore.
In this bed I've exploded each grief into her body, one by one,
until they came loose: the drinking, the failed marriages and jobs,
the weight of my children pressing me down.

There must be some kindness I could bring
to her dream now, listening to her breath unwind
in the small room and wishing I had never hurt anyone.
What still country have I come to,
where the long grass bends under the animals
when they lie down, emptied of suffering?
What slow river flows beneath her forehead,
the petals of her ears adrift in the auburn hair,
gathering darkness?

DARK HARVEST

For Annie

You can come to me in the evening,
        with the fingers of former lovers
fastened in your hair and their ghost lips
        opening over your body.
They can be philosophers or musicians in long coats and colored sho
and they can be smarter than I am,
        whispering to each other
                when they look at us.
You can come walking toward my window after dusk
        when I can't see past the lamplight in the glass,
when the chipped .plates rattle on the counter
        and the cinders
dance on the cross-ties under the wheels of southbound freights.
Bring children if you want, and the long wounds of sisters
        branching away
                behind you toward the sea.
Bring your mother's tense distracted face
                and the shoulders of plane mechanics
slumped in the Naugahyde booths of the airport diner,
        waiting for you to bring their eggs.

I'll bring all the bottles of gin I drank by myself
        and my cracked mouth opened partway
as I slept in the back of my blue Impala
                        dreaming of spiders.
I won't forget the lines running deeply
        in the cheeks of the Polish landlady
who wouldn't let the cops upstairs,
        the missing ring finger of the machinist from Spenard
whose money I stole after he passed out to go downtown in a cab

and look for whores,
        or the trembling lower jaw of my son, watching me
back my motorcycle from his mother's driveway one last time,
        the ribbons and cone-shaped birthday hats
scattered on the lawn,
                        the rain coming down like broken glass.

We'll go out under the stars and sit together on the ground
        and there will be enough to eat for everybody.
They can sleep on my couches and rug,
                        and the next day
I'll go to work, stepping easily across the scaffolding, feeding
the cable gently into the new pipes on the roof,
                        and dreaming
like St Francis of the still dark rocks
that disappear under the morning tide,
                        only to climb back into the light,
sea-rimed, salt-blotched, their patched webs of algae
blazing with flies in the sun.

WAKING UP AFTER READING PROUST

Maybe the heart decides while we sleep
what to remember
and the lights of a coal truck
sweeping our walls at midnight
will revisit us as an angel's face
we have already known.

Last week my son trod the dusty stage
of the living room carpet, secretly proud
in Egyptian dress, an elfin scribe to the Pharoah,
his mother's bracelets jangling
on thin forearms as he held up the reed pen
fashioned from wire and thread, the heiroglyphs for "water",
and the map copied out on shirt cardboard
to describe the Nile at flood.

I wondered if April's hennaed dusk
would leave its soft stain in his memory
as he reckoned the scribe's tasks on pale fingers:
keeping track of taxes and marriages, births, deaths,
and bushels of wheat; charting the arable land
of the kingdom, mapping the boundaries that disappeared
under the river each spring.

Everything I wanted then was close at hand:
the juice glass glowing like a lamp behind him,
the smell of onions deepening over the stove,
dark violin phrases twisting from the radio into the air.
I remembered the resinous shadows under the lid
of the cedar chest where my grandmother kept
the toys: the cowboy hat, the wooden sword,
the chipped hull of the plaster sailboat; and the winter light
ebbing away through the elms on Montgomery Avenue.

And maybe the brown pond gleaming
like an amniotic veil
under the arbor at Swann's estate
leads down to that darker ocean Jung says belongs
to everyone. Over the deep-sea fracture zones
where the gods jostle and shove,
its tides keep bearing the fragments up
into more peaceful water:

hawthorne cluster and village steeple,
the madeleine soaked in lime-blossom tea,
all shining with mud and phosphorus
on the dream's brief shoreline,
before the waves close over us again.

ACKNOWLEDGEMENTS

Grateful acknowledgement is made to the following journals and anthologies in which some of these poems first appeared:

Alaska Quarterly Review: "My Father and Thomas Wyatt in Hefka's Bar", "At Bay Meadows with Robert Herrick"
Caesura: "The Wayward Carpenter's Apprentice"
CrossConnect: "The Oaks Card Club"
DoubleTake: "Ed's Auto Repair"
Fish Dance: "Deck Boss"
Jacaranda Review: "Hansel and Gretel's Father"
Manoa: "Poem for a New Girlfriend," "Listener," "Near the Continental Divide," "Selling Out at the Top of the World"
Many Mountains Moving: "Telephone Repairman," "Sole Custody"
Mudfish: "Kung Fu"
Nebraska Review: "Names I'd Forgotten"
New Letters: "Family Therapy," "Twentieth Century Landscapes"
Passages North: "Young Mother"
Pearl: "Fat City"
Ploughshares: "Outside Monterey"
Poetry International: "Heart Attack"
Prairie Schooner: "Keats' Shadow"
Red Rock Review: "Lightnin' Hopkins Returns Home"
Shenandoah: "Fiber Optics"
Talking River Review: "Love Pirates"
33 Review: "Midlife"
TriQuarterly: "Waking Up after Reading Proust"
Willow Springs: "Spanish Blues"

"Midlife" appears in the anthology *Outsiders*, Milkweed Editions, 1999.
"Tax Man" appears in *A Richer Harvest: Literature of Work from the Pacific Northwest*, Oregon State University Press, 1999, and "Twentieth Century Landscapes" appears in *Hard Love: Writings on Violence and Intimacy*, Queen of Swords Press, 1997.

Special thanks to the Mountain Writers' Center and Oregon Literary Arts. Thanks to the installers at Voicepro, to David and the crew of the Tanglewood Six. Thanks also to Kim Addonizio, Diana O'Hehir, Garrett Hongo, Madeline DeFrees, Philip Levine, Steve Torre and Christopher Howell. And especially to John-Roger, Herman Bracey, and Dorianne Laux.